Mastering
Investing for Starters
2024 Insights

*Fast-Track Your Wealth-Your Ultimate Handbook to
Understand the Stock Market in 2024 for Immediate Gains
and a Secure Financial Future*

WAYNE WHITE

Table Of Contents

Why This Book Matters

Navigating the Wealth Frontier

In the vast landscape of financial literature, "Mastering Investing for Starters: 2024 Insights" stands as a beacon, guiding you through the intricacies of investing with purpose and precision. Why does this book matter? It transcends the conventional investment guides by offering not just knowledge but a transformative journey. Here's why it matters:

Empowerment through Knowledge:

This book demystifies the complexities of investing, providing you with a comprehensive understanding of the financial landscape. Knowledge is the key to empowerment, and this book equips you with the tools to navigate the wealth frontier with confidence.

Holistic Approach to Wealth Building:

Beyond mere financial gains, this book emphasizes mindful wealth-building. It encourages you to align your investments with your values, fostering a sense of purpose and fulfillment in your financial journey.

Adaptability in a Changing World:

In the dynamic world of finance, staying informed is crucial. "Mastering Investing for Starters" provides insights and strategies tailored to the current market trends of 2024, ensuring that you are not just a passive observer but an active participant in the evolution of the financial landscape.

A Lifelong Companion:

This book isn't a one-time read; it's a lifelong companion. With continuous updates and access to online resources, it grows with you. It's not just about mastering investing for starters; it's about evolving into a seasoned investor with each passing year.

INTRODUCTION

The Journey of Alex and the Wealth Compass

In a bustling city, amidst the flurry of daily life, lived Alex – a young professional with aspirations as vast as the horizon. Fresh out of college, armed with dreams of financial independence, Alex was eager to navigate the perplexing world of investments. But like many in this vibrant city, Alex faced a daunting challenge – the uncertainty of where to start in the vast landscape of finance.

Alex's quest for financial knowledge began with a serendipitous encounter. It was a bright Monday morning when Alex stumbled upon a weathered book tucked away in a corner of an old bookstore. Its title, "Mastering Investing for Starters: 2024 Insights," called out like a promise of untold riches. Little did Alex know, this book would be the key to unlocking a world of wealth and possibilities.

As Alex flipped through the pages, each chapter seemed like a treasure trove of wisdom waiting to be unearthed. The journey began with the basics, as if laying the sturdy bricks for a formidable fortress. The fundamentals of stocks, bonds, and funds were demystified in a language that resonated with Alex's eager mind.

But this was no ordinary book; it was a gateway to the future. Chapter by chapter, Alex delved deeper, discovering the transformative power of technology in investing. The world of automated trading strategies and tech-driven approaches to wealth building unfolded like a map to a hidden treasure.

With each turn of the page, Alex explored the globe through the lens of global market mastery. The book revealed secrets to diversifying investments across continents, painting a canvas of possibilities beyond local boundaries.

In the midst of real-time market insights and strategies to navigate volatility, Alex found solace. The fears that once clouded the path to financial growth began to dissipate. Armed with proven techniques to mitigate risks, Alex forged ahead with newfound confidence.

But the true magic lay in the stories within. The book was more than just words; it was a chorus of voices from industry titans. Their tales of triumph, their insights into the markets, and their unwavering spirit became guiding stars in Alex's journey.

As the chapters unfolded, each page echoed the aspirations of a community bound by a desire for financial success. Alex discovered a network of like-minded individuals within the book's pages – a community-driven learning hub offering support, camaraderie, and shared knowledge.

The journey didn't end with wealth accumulation; it transcended into a realm of purpose. The book opened doors to mindful wealth building, emphasizing values and conscious investing, aligning wealth with aspirations for a better world.

With every chapter, Alex's understanding deepened, evolving from a novice investor to a master strategist. The book wasn't just a manual; it was a lifelong companion, offering continuous learning, evolving strategies, and a vision of the future of finance.

As Alex closed the book, a sense of empowerment surged within. It wasn't just about mastering investments; it was about mastering a future of financial abundance, painted with aspirations and fueled by knowledge.

Dear reader, welcome to "Mastering Investing for Starters: 2024 Insights." Join us on a journey through the story of Alex and the wealth compass, as we navigate the vast frontier of finance together. This isn't just a book; it's a transformative experience waiting to be embraced.

What is Investing?

Investing is not merely a financial transaction; it's a deliberate and strategic allocation of resources to generate wealth over time. It involves:

Allocation of Capital:

- Identifying opportunities to allocate your capital, whether in stocks, bonds, real estate, or other assets.

Risk Management:

- Assessing and mitigating risks associated with investments to protect your capital and potential returns.

Long-Term Wealth Accumulation:

- Viewing investments as a vehicle for long-term wealth accumulation rather than short-term gains.

Purposeful Decision-Making:

- Making informed decisions based on thorough research, market trends, and a clear understanding of your financial goals.

Why Investing?

Investing is a powerful tool for wealth creation and financial security. Here's why it's a crucial aspect of your financial journey:

Wealth Growth:

✓ Investing has the potential to grow your wealth over time, outpacing inflation and traditional savings accounts.

Financial Freedom:

✓ Successful investing can lead to financial independence, providing the freedom to pursue your passions and live life on your terms.

Retirement Planning:

✓ Investing is a cornerstone of effective retirement planning, ensuring a comfortable and secure post-working life.

Achieving Financial Goals:

✓ Whether it's buying a home, funding education, or starting a business, investing provides the means to achieve your financial aspirations.

Unmasking Investment Fallacies: Shatter the Myths

Myth: Investing is Only for the Wealthy:

Reality: Anyone can start investing, regardless of their income. There are various investment options suitable for different financial situations.

Myth: Investing is Like Gambling:

Reality: Unlike gambling, investing involves careful analysis, research, and strategic decision-making. It's about managing risks and making informed choices.

Myth: You Need a Financial Background to Invest:

Reality: While financial knowledge is beneficial, it's not a prerequisite. This book is designed for beginners, providing a step-by-step guide to understanding and mastering investing.

Myth: Timing the Market is the Key to Success:

Reality: Successful investing is about time in

the market, not timing the market. Consistency and a long-term perspective often yield better results than attempting to predict short-term fluctuations.

"Mastering Investing for Starters: 2024 Insights" is not just a book; it's a tool for transformation, a gateway to financial empowerment, and a source of wisdom that debunks common myths, providing you with the knowledge and confidence to embark on your journey to financial mastery.

Navigating the Wealth Frontier

Welcome to the forefront of financial empowerment – a journey into the heart of wealth creation and investment mastery. In "Mastering Investing for Starters: 2024 Insights," we embark on a transformative exploration designed for the modern investor, blending timeless principles with cutting-edge strategies to pave the way for immediate gains and a secure financial future.

In the dynamic landscape of 2024, the allure of wealth creation is more tantalizing than ever, beckoning both novice investors and seasoned professionals to navigate the intricate pathways of the financial world. This book is your compass, your guide through the vast terrain of investment possibilities, tailored to meet the unique needs and aspirations of a diverse audience.

Foundations for Success: Chapter 1-5

Our journey begins with the fundamentals in Chapters 1 to 5, where we lay the groundwork for your financial triumph. From decoding the intricacies of stocks, bonds, and funds to unraveling the mysteries of real-time market insights, this section ensures you build a rock-solid foundation, arming you with the knowledge needed to confidently step into the world of investments.

Embracing the Future: Chapter 6-9

Chapters 6 to 9 propel you into the future of investing, where technology and automation are your allies. Discover the power of AI-driven strategies, glean wisdom from industry titans through exclusive interviews, and craft a personalized investment roadmap that aligns with your unique financial goals. It's not just about investing; it's about investing with foresight and purpose.

Community and Conscious Investing: Chapter 9-10

Beyond the individual journey, Chapters 9 and 10 introduce you to the power of community-driven learning and mindful wealth building. Join a thriving community of like-minded individuals, engage in interactive forums, and explore strategies that align your investments with ethical and sustainable practices. This is not merely a guide; it's an invitation to be part of a movement toward conscious wealth creation.

As we navigate this wealth frontier together, remember that this book is more than just a manual. It's a companion on your financial journey, offering real-world insights, expert perspectives, and a roadmap to financial mastery. Whether you're a novice investor, a tech enthusiast, or someone eager to embrace the global markets, "Mastering Investing for Starters: 2024 Insights" is crafted to meet you where you are and propel you toward the financial future you desire.

In the realm of investments, knowledge is not static; it's a living, breathing entity that evolves with the markets. In Chapter 11, we dive into the psychology of wealth, unraveling the emotional complexities that often accompany financial decisions. Understanding and mastering the psychological aspects of investing are crucial steps toward achieving sustained success.

As we progress to Chapter 12, we explore the often-overlooked yet immensely significant realm of tax-efficient investing. Here, we equip you with strategies to maximize your gains while minimizing the impact of taxes on your hard-earned wealth. It's not just about what you earn; it's about what you keep.

Our journey takes an ethical turn in Chapter 13, where we delve into sustainable and impact investing. Discover how your investments can not only yield financial returns but also contribute to positive societal and environmental changes. It's a powerful way to align your wealth-building endeavors with your values.

In Chapter 14, we decipher the art of market timing and seasonal trends. Recognizing opportune moments and understanding market cycles become tools in your arsenal, allowing you to make informed decisions based on the rhythm of the financial world.

Real estate, often considered a cornerstone of diversified portfolios, takes center stage in Chapter 15. We explore the intricacies of real estate investments, providing insights on balancing your portfolio with property assets.

Chapter 16 addresses a topic often deemed a distant concern – retirement. For young professionals, crafting a roadmap for early retirement becomes an empowering endeavor. It's about envisioning a future of financial freedom and taking actionable steps to make that vision a reality.

As we venture further into the complexities of investing, Chapter 17 introduces advanced trading strategies. Options trading, day trading, and other advanced tactics are unveiled with a focus on mitigating risks while exploring avenues for enhanced returns.

In Chapter 18, we plunge into the digital frontier of finance with a comprehensive guide to mastering cryptocurrency investments. As digital assets reshape the financial landscape, understanding and integrating cryptocurrencies into your portfolio become essential for staying ahead.

Chapter 19 takes a holistic approach, addressing financial wellness and lifestyle design. Your wealth-building journey isn't just about numbers on a screen; it's about designing a lifestyle that reflects your financial success and aligns with your aspirations.

Our journey into the future concludes in Chapter 20, where we explore emerging trends shaping the financial markets. Anticipating these trends equips you with the foresight needed to position yourself for success in the evolving landscape of investing.

As we conclude this introduction, consider this book not just as a guide but as a companion on your ongoing journey to financial mastery. It's not about reaching a destination; it's about evolving, adapting, and thriving in the ever-changing world of finance. Welcome to "Mastering Investing for Starters: 2024 Insights" – your passport to a future of financial abundance.

So, buckle up as we embark on this transformative odyssey into the world of investing. Your journey to mastering the art of investment in 2024 and beyond starts now.

CHAPTER 1

Investing Fundamentals for Novices

As your guide through the intricate world of investment, I'm here to provide expert insights into the foundational principles that will shape your journey towards financial mastery. In this chapter, we unravel the intricacies of investing, focusing on fundamental elements that form the bedrock of wealth creation for novices like yourself.

Understanding the Basics: Stocks, Bonds, and Funds

Deciphering Stock Selection:

Navigating the stock market involves more than mere chance—it requires informed decision-making. In this consultation, we delve into the art of stock selection, exploring advanced strategies such as fundamental analysis and technical indicators. Uncover the nuances of various stock types and how to align them with your risk tolerance and investment objectives.

Strategic Bond Portfolio Construction:

Bonds, often considered the steady anchors in an investment portfolio, demand a strategic approach. We'll explore advanced bond portfolio construction techniques, including yield curve analysis and credit risk assessment. Understand how to customize your bond investments to optimize returns while managing risk effectively.

Mastering Fund Allocation:

Beyond the surface-level understanding, we'll embark on an in-depth exploration of mutual funds and ETFs. Learn sophisticated techniques for optimizing fund allocations, including tactical asset allocation and factor investing. This consultation will empower you to create a diversified and resilient portfolio through astute fund selection and strategic weightings.

Building a Solid Financial Foundation for Beginners

Strategic Budgeting for Wealth Accumulation:

Budgeting isn't just about tracking expenses; it's a strategic tool for wealth accumulation. In this session, we'll delve into advanced budgeting techniques, such as zero-based budgeting and the 50/30/20 rule. Uncover how strategic budgeting can amplify your savings, setting the stage for impactful investments.

Advanced Emergency Fund Strategies:

Your financial safety net should not only provide a cushion but also serve as a strategic asset. Discover advanced strategies for managing emergency funds, including optimizing for tax efficiency and incorporating liquid investments. This consultation will guide you in turning your emergency fund into a dynamic financial resource.

Strategic Financial Goal Setting:

Setting financial goals is an art that extends beyond mere aspirations. We'll explore advanced techniques for defining and prioritizing your financial goals. Understand how to create a dynamic goal-setting framework that adapts to changing circumstances, ensuring your investments align seamlessly with your evolving objectives.

By delving into these advanced concepts, you'll elevate your understanding of investing beyond the basics. This expert consultation is designed to equip you with the tools and knowledge needed to navigate the intricate landscape of financial markets with precision and foresight. As we progress through this chapter, you'll emerge not only with a comprehensive understanding of investment fundamentals but also with the strategic acumen to navigate the markets as a seasoned investor. Get ready to elevate your investment journey to new heights.

CHAPTER 2

The Tech-Driven Future of Investing

In the ever-evolving landscape of financial markets, Chapter 2 propels us into the future of investing—a realm where technology takes center stage, empowering investors with unprecedented tools and strategies. Join me as we explore the exciting frontier of automated trading strategies and learn how to seamlessly integrate technology for efficient and intelligent investments.

Exploring Automated Trading Strategies

Understanding Algorithmic Trading:

Automated trading, powered by sophisticated algorithms, has revolutionized the way we approach financial markets.

This section provides an in-depth exploration of algorithmic trading, unraveling the complexities of trading strategies executed by computers. Gain insights into high-frequency trading, quantitative analysis, and algorithmic decision-making processes that drive modern financial markets.

Strategies for Success:

Not all automated strategies are created equal. This segment delves into proven automated trading strategies, ranging from trend following to mean reversion. Explore how algorithmic traders capitalize on market inefficiencies and price patterns, and gain a deep understanding of the risk management principles that underpin successful automated trading.

The Rise of Robo-Advisors:

Robo-advisors have emerged as powerful tools for individual investors. Learn how these automated platforms leverage algorithms to create and manage diversified portfolios based on investors' risk tolerance and financial goals. Understand the benefits and limitations of robo-advisors, and discover how they democratize access to sophisticated investment strategies.

Integrating Technology for Efficient and Smart Investments

Big Data and Predictive Analytics:

The era of big data has transformed the investment landscape. Explore how predictive analytics, fueled by vast datasets, empower investors to make data-driven decisions. From sentiment analysis to machine learning models, discover how advanced analytics can provide a competitive edge in forecasting market trends and identifying investment opportunities.

Smart Order Routing and Execution:

Efficient trade execution is crucial in the fast-paced world of financial markets. This segment delves into smart order routing systems, examining how technology optimizes trade execution for speed and cost-effectiveness. Gain insights into algorithms that navigate order books, minimizing slippage and maximizing execution efficiency.

Blockchain and Cryptocurrencies:

The disruptive force of blockchain technology extends beyond cryptocurrencies. Understand how blockchain enhances transparency, security, and efficiency in financial transactions. Explore the impact of decentralized finance (DeFi) on traditional investment models and the potential of blockchain to reshape the future of investing.

As we traverse the tech-driven future of investing, you'll not only grasp the intricacies of automated trading but also gain the skills to harness technology for intelligent and efficient investments. This chapter is your gateway to a realm where algorithms, big data, and emerging technologies converge to redefine the very essence of modern investing. Get ready to embrace the future with a strategic fusion of technological prowess and financial acumen.

Chapter 3

Global Market Mastery

Welcome to a chapter that transcends borders and propels you into the dynamic world of global market mastery. In this exploration, we will unravel the strategies and insights necessary to navigate international markets with confidence and master the art of portfolio diversification on a global scale.

Navigating International Markets with Confidence

Understanding Global Market Dynamics:

Global markets are interconnected, and understanding their dynamics is paramount. Delve into the complexities of international markets, exploring the impact of geopolitical events, economic indicators, and currency fluctuations on global investments. Gain insights into the factors that shape market sentiment across borders.

Regional Market Analysis:

Each region possesses unique opportunities and challenges. This section provides a comprehensive analysis of major global markets, from established financial hubs to emerging economies. Understand the regulatory landscapes, cultural nuances, and economic trends that influence investment dynamics in regions such as Asia, Europe, North America, and beyond.

Strategies for Mitigating Risks in Global Investing:

Global investing comes with its share of risks. Learn advanced strategies for mitigating risks in international portfolios, including currency risk management, geopolitical risk analysis, and diversification techniques tailored for a global context. Discover how to navigate uncertainties and seize opportunities in diverse markets.

Diversifying Your Portfolio on a Global Scale

The Power of Asset Class Diversification:

Diversification is the cornerstone of risk management. Explore advanced techniques for diversifying across asset classes on a global scale. From equities and fixed income to alternative investments, understand how a well-balanced and globally diversified portfolio can enhance returns and minimize risk.

Alternative Investments Across Borders:

Beyond traditional assets, this segment explores the world of alternative investments on a global stage. From real estate and private equity to commodities and venture capital, uncover how alternative investments can add a layer of diversification and potentially enhance your portfolio's risk-adjusted returns.

Strategic Considerations for Global Portfolio Allocation:

Crafting a globally diversified portfolio requires strategic allocation. This section provides insights into asset allocation models, risk-return optimization, and tailoring portfolio strategies to your investment goals. Understand how to align your portfolio with global economic trends and position yourself for long-term success.

As we embark on this journey of global market mastery, you will gain not only the knowledge to navigate international markets confidently but also the strategic insights to diversify your portfolio across borders. This chapter is your guide to a global investment landscape where opportunities abound, and with the right expertise, you can capitalize on the richness of diverse markets. Get ready to elevate your investment strategy to a truly global scale, positioning yourself for success in the interconnected world of finance.

CHAPTER 4

Real-Time Market Insights

Welcome to the heartbeat of the financial world, where real-time market insights form the bedrock of informed decision-making. In this chapter, we'll explore the transformative power of up-to-the-minute trends and analysis, providing you with the tools to not only stay ahead but to capitalize on the latest opportunities that the dynamic year of 2024 presents.

The Power of Up-to-the-Minute Trends and Analysis

Harnessing Real-Time Data:

In the fast-paced realm of financial markets, real-time data is your most valuable asset. Discover the sources and tools that provide instant access to market movements, price fluctuations, and breaking news. Learn how to leverage real-time data to make timely and well-informed decisions, giving you a competitive edge in today's rapidly changing landscape.

Advanced Technical Analysis:

Technical analysis is elevated to new heights when conducted in real-time. Explore advanced technical indicators and chart patterns that thrive on the immediacy of market data. From Fibonacci retracements to Ichimoku clouds, this section equips you with the skills to interpret real-time charts and identify potential entry and exit points with precision.

Sentiment Analysis in Real Time:

Market sentiment can shift swiftly, and being attuned to these changes is essential. Dive into the world of sentiment analysis tools, social media monitoring, and news sentiment indicators. Understand how to gauge the mood of the market in real-time, allowing you to anticipate trends and position yourself strategically.

How to Capitalize on the Latest Opportunities in 2024

Identifying Emerging Trends:

The year 2024 holds a tapestry of opportunities waiting to be unveiled. This section provides insights into identifying and capitalizing on emerging trends across various sectors. From technological advancements to geopolitical shifts, gain a forward-looking perspective that enables you to position your investments ahead of the curve.

Strategies for Rapid Decision-Making:

In a market where every second counts, the ability to make rapid decisions is paramount. Discover strategies for swift decision-making, including pre-defined trading plans, scenario analysis, and setting up alerts for key market events. Learn how to stay composed under pressure and execute timely trades to capitalize on fleeting opportunities.

Real-Time Risk Management:

Capitalizing on opportunities goes hand-in-hand with effective risk management. Explore advanced risk management techniques tailored for real-time trading. From setting dynamic stop-loss orders to employing options strategies for hedging, this section ensures that your pursuit of opportunities is accompanied by a robust risk mitigation framework.

As we delve into the realm of real-time market insights, you'll not only grasp the significance of staying current but also acquire the skills to transform information into actionable intelligence. This chapter is your gateway to a future where seizing opportunities in the ever-evolving financial landscape is not just a possibility but a strategic advantage. Get ready to ride the waves of real-time market dynamics and position yourself at the forefront of opportunity in 2024.

CHAPTER 5

Mitigating Risks in a Volatile Market

Welcome to a chapter that serves as your shield in the unpredictable terrain of financial markets. In this exploration, we'll delve into proven techniques for safeguarding your investments and strategic approaches to shield your portfolio amidst the ebbs and flows of a volatile market.

Proven Techniques for Safeguarding Your Investments

Portfolio Diversification Reimagined:

Diversification is a cornerstone of risk mitigation, but in this chapter, we take it a step further. Explore advanced diversification strategies that go beyond traditional asset classes. From incorporating uncorrelated assets to dynamically rebalancing your portfolio, these techniques enhance your ability to withstand volatility and reduce exposure to specific risks.

Options Strategies for Hedging:

Options provide a powerful toolkit for risk management. Dive into the world of options strategies, including protective puts, covered calls, and collars. Learn how to strategically use options to hedge against downside risk while maintaining the potential for upside gains. This section equips you with the skills to navigate the options market for effective risk mitigation.

Dynamic Risk Parity Models:

Traditional portfolio allocation models may fall short in volatile markets. Discover the principles of dynamic risk parity, a sophisticated approach that allocates assets based on their risk contributions rather than nominal weights. Understand how this dynamic framework adapts to changing market conditions, optimizing your portfolio's risk-return profile.

Strategies to Protect Your Portfolio in Changing Market Conditions

Tactical Asset Allocation:

Market conditions are dynamic, and your investment strategy should be too. Uncover the principles of tactical asset allocation, where strategic adjustments are made based on prevailing market trends. Learn how to identify signals that trigger shifts in your asset allocation, ensuring your portfolio remains resilient in the face of changing market conditions.

Active Risk Management:

In a volatile market, being proactive is key. This section explores active risk management techniques, including setting dynamic stop-loss orders, utilizing trailing stops, and employing volatility-based indicators. Understand how to assess risk in real-time and adjust your portfolio's exposure to align with your risk tolerance and market conditions.

Stress Testing Your Portfolio:

Prepare for the worst while aiming for the best through stress testing. Learn how to simulate various market scenarios to assess how your portfolio would perform under stress. Identify vulnerabilities, adjust your strategy accordingly, and fortify your portfolio against unforeseen events.

As we navigate through the strategies in this chapter, you'll not only fortify your understanding of risk mitigation but also gain practical insights into safeguarding your investments in the face of market volatility. This chapter is your strategic guide to weathering storms, ensuring that your portfolio not only endures but emerges stronger in the dynamic and ever-changing landscape of financial markets. Get ready to build resilience and fortitude into your investment approach.

CHAPTER 6

Wisdom from the Titans – Expert Interviews

Step into the inner sanctum of investment wisdom as we unlock the insights, experiences, and lessons from industry titans. Chapter 6 is your exclusive pass to the minds of financial gurus, providing you with unparalleled access to their exclusive insights, real success stories, and the invaluable lessons that have shaped their path to prosperity.

Exclusive Insights from Industry Leaders

In-Depth Interviews with Market Maestros:

This chapter features in-depth interviews with industry leaders who have not only weathered the storms of financial markets but have emerged as pioneers. Explore conversations with renowned fund managers, seasoned analysts, and visionaries who share their unique perspectives on market trends, investment strategies, and the ever-evolving landscape of finance.

Unraveling Investment Philosophies:

Each interview delves into the core investment philosophies that have guided these titans to success. From value investing to growth strategies, gain a nuanced understanding of diverse approaches that have stood the test of time. This section serves as a treasure trove of philosophies that you can adapt and integrate into your own investment framework.

Forecasting Market Trends with Precision:

These interviews aren't just retrospectives; they offer a forward-looking lens into market trends. Learn how these titans forecast market movements, identify emerging opportunities, and position themselves strategically for the future. Gain insights into the thought processes that guide their investment decisions in the fast-paced world of finance.

Navigating Market Challenges:

Success stories are often born out of overcoming challenges. Hear firsthand accounts of how these industry leaders navigated through market crises, economic downturns, and unforeseen obstacles. Uncover the strategies and resilience that propelled them forward, offering valuable lessons for navigating your own investment journey.

Striking the Balance Between Risk and Reward:

Risk management is a central theme in these interviews. Explore how these titans strike the delicate balance between risk and reward, making decisions that align with their risk tolerance and long-term objectives. Gain insights into risk assessment, strategic hedging, and the art of making calculated investment choices.

Life Lessons Beyond Finance:

Beyond the charts and balance sheets, these interviews touch on life lessons that have contributed to success. Discover the habits, mindset, and personal philosophies that have played a pivotal role in the lives of these titans. From time management to the importance of continuous learning, these life lessons offer a holistic perspective on success.

As you immerse yourself in the wisdom from the titans, you'll not only gain a front-row seat to the experiences of industry leaders but also extract actionable insights that can shape your own journey. This chapter is your exclusive backstage pass to the minds of those who have achieved greatness in the financial realm. Get ready to be inspired, informed, and empowered by the wisdom of the titans.

CHAPTER 7

Automated Investing Tactics for Beginners

Embark on a journey into the future of investing, where technology takes the lead and empowers beginners to implement automated trading strategies with ease. In this chapter, we explore the transformative world of automated investing, demystifying the process and showcasing how Artificial Intelligence (AI) can be leveraged for effortless gains.

Implementing Automated Trading Strategies with Ease

Introduction to Automated Investing:

For beginners, automated investing might seem like a complex endeavor. This section acts as your gateway, providing a comprehensive introduction to the world of automated trading. Understand the fundamental concepts, the role of algorithms, and how automation can streamline your investment approach.

Choosing the Right Automated Platforms:

Not all automated platforms are created equal. Navigate through the myriad of options and learn how to choose the right automated trading platform for your needs. Explore user-friendly interfaces, robust backtesting capabilities, and the integration of essential tools that facilitate seamless execution of automated strategies.

Building and Testing Your Automated Strategy:

Take the reins of automation by learning how to build and test your own strategies. Dive into the process of creating algorithms that align with your risk tolerance and investment goals. Understand the importance of backtesting to ensure your strategy is robust and well-calibrated for real-market conditions.

Leveraging AI for Effortless Gains

Understanding the Role of AI in Investing:

Demystify the role of Artificial Intelligence in investing. Explore how AI algorithms analyze vast datasets, identify patterns, and make data-driven predictions. Gain insights into the capabilities of machine learning models in adapting to market changes and refining investment strategies over time.

AI-Powered Portfolio Management:

Discover the transformative power of AI in portfolio management. From dynamic asset allocation to risk management, understand how AI can optimize your portfolio for maximum returns while minimizing exposure to volatility. This section provides actionable insights on integrating AI into your investment decision-making process.

Exploring Algorithmic Trading Strategies:

Delve into the realm of algorithmic trading and explore specific strategies that beginners can leverage. From trend-following algorithms to mean-reversion models, understand the nuances of each strategy and how AI can enhance their effectiveness. Gain confidence in implementing these strategies with a beginner-friendly approach.

As you navigate through the automated investing tactics presented in this chapter, you'll not only demystify the complexities but also gain the tools and knowledge needed to leverage AI for effortless gains. This chapter serves as a stepping stone for beginners, offering a clear roadmap into the exciting world of automated investing. Get ready to embrace the future of finance, where technology becomes your ally in the pursuit of financial success.

CHAPTER 8

Crafting Your Personal Investment Roadmap

Welcome to the heart of your financial journey—a chapter dedicated to crafting a personalized investment roadmap that aligns with your unique goals and aspirations. In this exploration, we'll delve into the art of tailoring strategies, ensuring they resonate with your individual financial landscape, and provide you with a roadmap for long-term success.

Tailoring Strategies for Unique Financial Goals

Defining Your Financial Goals:

Every successful journey begins with a destination in mind. In this section, we'll guide you through the process of defining your financial goals. Whether it's saving for a dream home, funding education, or achieving early retirement, understanding your aspirations sets the stage for crafting a tailored investment strategy.

Aligning Investments with Objectives:

Once your goals are crystal clear, the next step is aligning your investments with these objectives. Learn how to categorize your goals based on timelines, risk tolerance, and expected returns. This tailored approach ensures that each investment serves a specific purpose in your overall financial plan.

Risk-Return Profiling:

No two investors are alike, and neither should their risk profiles be. Explore the intricacies of risk-return profiling, allowing you to tailor your investment strategy to match your comfort level with risk. Whether you're a conservative investor seeking stability or an aggressive investor chasing high returns, this section guides you in finding the right balance.

Time Horizons and Investment Strategies:

Understand the critical relationship between time horizons and investment strategies. Whether you're planning for short-term goals like a vacation or long-term goals like retirement, learn how to match the appropriate investment vehicles and strategies to the timeframes of your objectives.

Periodic Review and Adjustments:

A successful investment roadmap is not static—it evolves. Explore the importance of periodic reviews and adjustments to ensure your investments stay aligned with your goals. Learn how to adapt your strategy in response to life changes, market conditions, and shifts in your financial landscape.

Integrating Tax-Efficient Strategies:

Efficiently managing taxes is a vital aspect of long-term success. This section introduces tax-efficient investment strategies, including the use of tax-advantaged accounts, strategic harvesting of capital gains, and optimizing your investment portfolio to minimize tax implications.

As you navigate through the intricacies of crafting your personal investment roadmap, you'll not only tailor strategies to your unique financial goals but also build a foundation for long-term success. This chapter acts as your guide, ensuring that your investment journey is not only purposeful but also adaptable, providing you with the tools to navigate the dynamic landscape of personal finance with confidence and precision. Get ready to shape a roadmap that leads you towards a prosperous financial future.

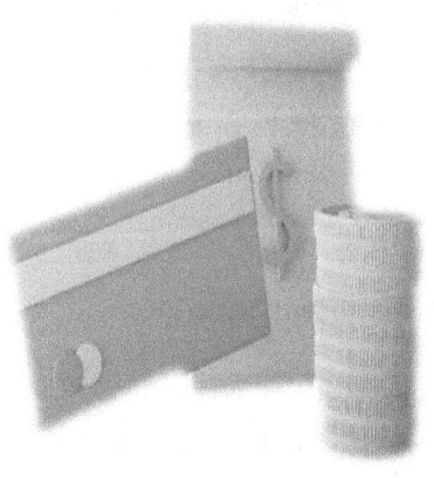

CHAPTER 9

Community-Driven Learning

Step into a chapter that transcends individual learning—a space where community-driven learning becomes the catalyst for collective growth. In Chapter 9, we explore the profound benefits of joining a thriving community of aspiring investors, immersing yourself in interactive forums that foster networking, support, and a shared journey towards financial mastery.

Joining a Thriving Community of Aspiring Investors

The Power of Collective Wisdom:

In the realm of investing, collective wisdom often outshines individual insights. Discover the transformative power of joining a community where investors of all levels converge. By tapping into a pool of diverse experiences, perspectives, and expertise, you gain a holistic understanding of the financial landscape.

Networking Opportunities:

Networking is not just a professional concept—it's a cornerstone of successful investing. Explore how joining a thriving investment community opens doors to networking opportunities. Connect with like-minded individuals, experienced investors, and industry professionals. This network becomes a valuable asset, providing insights, opportunities, and potential collaborations.

Sharing Success Stories and Challenges:

In a community-driven setting, success stories and challenges become communal experiences. Share your triumphs and setbacks, and learn from others who have walked similar paths. Celebrate victories, gain inspiration, and navigate challenges more effectively by drawing on the collective knowledge and support of the community.

Virtual Roundtables and Q&A Sessions:

Immerse yourself in interactive forums that bring learning to life. Participate in virtual roundtables where members discuss current market trends, share investment strategies, and seek collective insights. Engage in Q&A sessions with industry experts, fostering an environment of continuous learning and real-time knowledge exchange.

Mentorship Programs:

Community-driven learning often includes mentorship programs, where seasoned investors guide those embarking on their financial journey. Explore the benefits of mentorship within the community, gaining personalized advice, feedback, and a roadmap crafted by someone who has navigated similar terrain.

Peer-to-Peer Learning Platforms:

In a community-driven learning environment, everyone is both a learner and a teacher. Explore peer-to-peer learning platforms where members share educational resources, research findings, and market analyses. This collaborative approach accelerates the learning curve for everyone involved.

As you delve into the world of community-driven learning in this chapter, you'll not only expand your knowledge base but also find a support system that propels your journey to financial mastery. This community becomes more than just a forum—it becomes a dynamic space where collective growth, shared insights, and mutual encouragement redefine the way you approach investing. Get ready to immerse yourself in a community where the journey towards financial success is a shared endeavor, and the possibilities for learning are limitless.

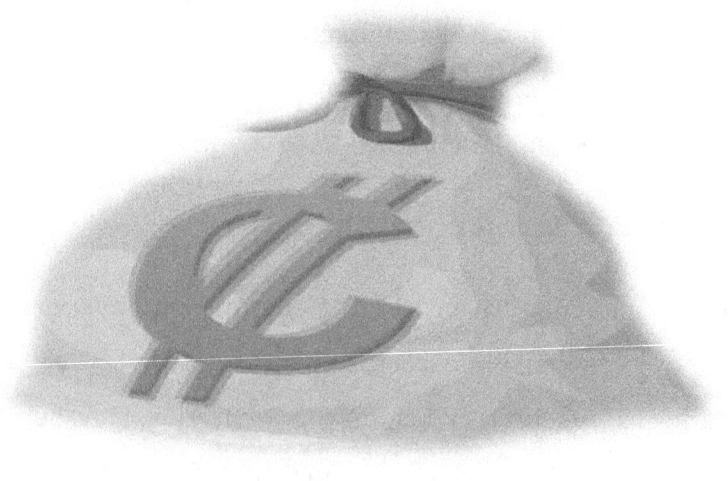

CHAPTER 10

Mindful Wealth Building

Welcome to a chapter that transcends traditional investment approaches—a space where investing becomes a conscious and purpose-driven endeavor. In Chapter 10, we explore the art of mindful wealth building, providing strategies for aligning your investments with your values, and fostering conscious and ethical wealth accumulation.

Investing with Purpose and Values

Defining Your Investment Philosophy:

Mindful wealth building begins with a clear understanding of your values. In this section, explore the process of defining your investment philosophy—a set of principles that guide your financial decisions. Understand how your values shape your approach to risk, return, and the impact your investments have on society and the environment.

Ethical Screening and Responsible Investing:

Dive into the world of ethical screening and responsible investing. Learn how to align your portfolio with companies and industries that resonate with your values. Discover the growing universe of sustainable investments, from environmentally conscious funds to those promoting social responsibility, and how they can form the bedrock of your mindful wealth-building strategy.

Impact Investing for Social Change:

Move beyond traditional returns and explore the realm of impact investing. Understand how your investments can contribute to positive social and environmental change. From supporting clean energy initiatives to investing in businesses with a focus on diversity and inclusion, this section empowers you to make a meaningful impact through your financial decisions.

Strategies for Conscious and Ethical Wealth Building

> *Evaluating Environmental, Social, and Governance (ESG) Factors:*

Explore the incorporation of Environmental, Social, and Governance (ESG) factors into your investment decisions. Understand how companies are evaluated based on their commitment to sustainability, ethical business practices, and corporate governance. Learn to use ESG metrics to guide your investment choices and contribute to a more sustainable future.

> *Community-Centric Investing:*

Mindful wealth building extends beyond individual gain— it encompasses the well-being of communities. Discover the principles of community-centric investing, where you direct capital towards projects and businesses that uplift local communities. Explore opportunities for impact in areas such as affordable housing, community development, and small business support.

➤ *Long-Term Value Creation:*

Mindful wealth building takes a long-term perspective, prioritizing sustained value creation over short-term gains. Explore strategies for long-term value creation, including patient investing in innovative companies, fostering sustainable business practices, and contributing to economic resilience.

As you navigate the terrain of mindful wealth building in this chapter, you'll not only align your investments with your values but also contribute to positive societal and environmental change. This chapter becomes your guide to a holistic approach to wealth accumulation—one that reflects your conscious choices and makes a positive impact on the world. Get ready to embark on a journey where your wealth-building strategy is not just financially sound but also ethically and socially responsible.

CHAPTER 11

The Psychology of Wealth

In Chapter 11, we delve into the complex and often underestimated realm of the psychology of wealth. Beyond numbers and charts, this chapter explores the emotional aspects of investing, providing insights into understanding and navigating the intricate interplay between the human mind and financial decisions. Learn how to overcome common psychological hurdles and cultivate a mindset conducive to long-term success.

Understanding the Emotional Aspects of Investing

The Role of Emotions in Financial Decision-Making:

Investing is not just a rational endeavor; it is profoundly influenced by emotions. In this section, explore the psychological underpinnings of financial decision-making. Understand how emotions such as fear, greed, and overconfidence can impact investment choices and learn strategies to navigate these emotions effectively.

The Influence of Behavioral Biases:

Behavioral biases are inherent to human psychology and can significantly impact investment outcomes. Delve into common biases such as loss aversion, recency bias, and herd mentality. Recognize how these biases shape decision-making and explore techniques to mitigate their influence on your investment strategy.

The Connection Between Risk Tolerance and Emotional Resilience:

Risk tolerance is not solely about numbers; it's deeply intertwined with emotional resilience. Learn how to assess your risk tolerance by considering not just financial factors but also your emotional capacity to withstand market fluctuations. Discover strategies for aligning your investment decisions with both your financial and emotional comfort levels.

Overcoming Common Psychological Hurdles for Success

Patience and Discipline in Investing:

Patience and discipline are the bedrock of successful investing. Understand the importance of cultivating a patient mindset and disciplined approach to withstand market volatility and stay committed to your long-term investment goals. Learn techniques to foster patience and resist the impulse to make impulsive decisions.

Building a Positive Investment Mindset:

Your mindset shapes your reality. Explore strategies for building a positive investment mindset that fosters resilience, adaptability, and a constructive outlook. Discover the power of positive affirmations, visualization, and gratitude in shaping your perception of wealth-building and overcoming setbacks.

Seeking Professional Guidance for Emotional Intelligence:

Recognizing the emotional aspects of investing is a crucial step towards success. Explore the benefits of seeking professional guidance, not only for financial expertise but also for emotional intelligence. Learn how financial advisors can provide support, guidance, and a grounded perspective during emotionally charged market conditions.

As you navigate through the psychology of wealth in this chapter, you'll gain a deeper understanding of the emotional dynamics that shape your financial decisions. Armed with this knowledge, you'll be better equipped to overcome common psychological hurdles and cultivate a mindset conducive to successful, resilient, and emotionally intelligent wealth building. Get ready to embark on a journey where the psychology of wealth becomes a powerful ally on your path to financial success.

CHAPTER 12

Tax-Efficient Investing

In Chapter 12, we embark on a strategic exploration of tax-efficient investing—a discipline that goes beyond maximizing gains to minimize tax implications. This chapter is your guide to crafting a tax-efficient portfolio management strategy, ensuring that you retain more of your hard-earned wealth and optimize your financial outcomes.

Maximizing Gains While Minimizing Tax Implications

Understanding the Tax Landscape:

Tax efficiency begins with a clear understanding of the tax landscape. In this section, explore the different types of taxes that can impact your investments, from capital gains taxes to dividend taxes. Gain insights into how changes in tax laws and regulations can shape your investment decisions.

Tax-Advantaged Accounts:

One of the cornerstones of tax-efficient investing is leveraging tax-advantaged accounts. Delve into the benefits of retirement accounts such as 401(k)s and IRAs, as well as other tax-advantaged vehicles. Learn how these accounts can shield your investments from immediate tax obligations and compound your wealth over time.

Strategies for Tax-Loss Harvesting:

Discover the art of tax-loss harvesting—a strategy that involves selling investments at a loss to offset gains and reduce taxable income. Learn how to identify opportunities for tax-loss harvesting, the rules governing this practice, and how it can enhance your overall tax efficiency.

Strategies for Tax-Efficient Portfolio Management

- *Asset Location Strategies:*

Asset location is a key determinant of tax efficiency. Explore strategies for optimal asset location, including the placement of tax-inefficient assets in tax-advantaged accounts and tax-efficient assets in taxable accounts. Learn how this approach can enhance after-tax returns and minimize the impact of taxes on your portfolio.

- *Managing Dividend and Interest Income:*

Dividend and interest income are integral components of many investment portfolios. This section delves into strategies for managing these income streams in a tax-efficient manner. Explore the benefits of dividend growth investing, tax-advantaged bond options, and techniques for minimizing the tax impact of interest income.

- *Tax-Efficient Withdrawal Strategies:*

As you transition from wealth accumulation to distribution, the strategy for withdrawing funds becomes crucial. Uncover tax-efficient withdrawal strategies that aim to minimize your tax liability during retirement. Explore techniques such as Roth IRA conversions, systematic withdrawal plans, and the strategic use of taxable and tax-advantaged accounts.

As you navigate through the intricacies of tax-efficient investing in this chapter, you'll not only gain a comprehensive understanding of the tax implications on your portfolio but also acquire the skills to strategically manage and optimize your investments from a tax perspective. This chapter becomes your roadmap to maximizing gains while minimizing the impact of taxes, ensuring that your wealth-building journey is not just lucrative but also tax-efficient. Get ready to unlock the full potential of your investments through strategic tax planning and management.

CHAPTER 13

Sustainable and Impact Investing

Embark on a transformative journey in Chapter 13 as we explore the realm of sustainable and impact investing. This chapter is your guide to incorporating Environmental, Social, and Governance (ESG) principles into your investment approach, enabling you to invest with a positive impact on both society and the environment.

Incorporating ESG Principles into Your Investment Approach

Understanding ESG:

Environmental, Social, and Governance (ESG) principles have emerged as guiding metrics for responsible and sustainable investing. In this section, gain a comprehensive understanding of what ESG entails. Explore how companies are evaluated based on their environmental practices, social impact, and governance structures.

ESG Integration into Investment Decisions:

Dive into the practical application of ESG principles in your investment decisions. Learn how to integrate ESG factors into your analysis of potential investments. Discover tools and metrics that assess a company's commitment to sustainability, social responsibility, and ethical governance, allowing you to align your portfolio with your values.

Impact of ESG on Risk and Return:

ESG considerations are not just about values—they have tangible impacts on risk and return. Explore how companies with strong ESG practices often exhibit lower risk profiles and, in some cases, outperform their counterparts. Understand the correlation between ESG and financial performance, allowing you to make informed and responsible investment choices.

Investing with a Positive Impact on Society and the Environment

Sustainable Investing Strategies:

Sustainable investing goes beyond minimizing harm; it actively seeks positive impact. Explore sustainable investing strategies that focus on supporting companies contributing to positive environmental and social change. From renewable energy initiatives to companies fostering diversity and inclusion, discover ways to align your investments with a sustainable future.

Impact Investing Across Asset Classes:

Impact investing spans various asset classes, providing a diverse range of opportunities to make a positive difference. Explore how impact investing extends beyond equities to include fixed income, real estate, and private equity. Learn how each asset class can contribute to positive societal and environmental outcomes.

Measuring Impact and Reporting:

Investors committed to sustainable and impact investing often seek transparency and accountability. Delve into the metrics and reporting frameworks used to measure the impact of investments. Understand how organizations disclose their ESG practices and impact metrics, empowering you to make informed decisions about the positive contributions of your portfolio.

As you navigate through the principles of sustainable and impact investing in this chapter, you'll not only align your investments with your values but also contribute to positive change on a broader scale. This chapter becomes your gateway to a financial journey where every investment decision is an opportunity to create a more sustainable and equitable world. Get ready to invest with purpose and make a positive impact through your financial choices.

CHAPTER 14

Market Timing and Seasonal Trends

Welcome to the intriguing realm of market timing and seasonal trends in Chapter 14. This chapter serves as your guide to recognizing favorable times for specific investments and leveraging seasonal trends for gains. Explore the nuances of timing within the market and discover how to align your investment strategy with the ebbs and flows of seasonal patterns.

Recognizing Favorable Times for Specific Investments

Understanding Market Cycles:

Markets move in cycles, and recognizing these patterns is a key element of successful market timing. In this section, delve into the stages of market cycles, from expansion to contraction. Understand the indicators and signals that mark each phase, empowering you to make informed decisions based on the prevailing market conditions.

Strategic Entry and Exit Points:

Market timing involves identifying strategic entry and exit points for investments. Learn how to analyze technical indicators, chart patterns, and economic data to pinpoint opportune moments to enter or exit positions. Explore both short-term and long-term timing strategies, allowing you to adapt your approach to different investment horizons.

Sector Rotation Strategies:

Not all sectors perform equally well at all times. Explore sector rotation strategies that involve shifting investments between different sectors based on economic and market conditions. Understand how sector analysis can help you allocate your portfolio to sectors poised for growth during specific phases of the economic cycle.

Seasonal Trends and How to Leverage Them for Gains

Introduction to Seasonal Trends:

Markets exhibit recurring patterns based on the calendar, known as seasonal trends. In this section, discover the concept of seasonal investing and how certain months or periods historically show consistent patterns. From the "January Effect" to the "Santa Claus Rally," grasp the fundamentals of leveraging seasonal trends for strategic gains.

Optimizing Asset Allocation Seasonally:

Seasonal trends extend beyond individual stocks to impact entire asset classes. Explore strategies for optimizing your asset allocation based on seasonal trends. Understand how different asset classes, such as equities, bonds, and commodities, may exhibit varying performance during specific seasons, allowing you to fine-tune your portfolio accordingly.

Weathering Seasonal Volatility:

Seasonal trends can introduce volatility, and understanding how to navigate this turbulence is essential. Learn how to weather seasonal volatility by incorporating risk management techniques. From adjusting position sizes to utilizing protective options strategies, this section equips you with the tools to navigate market fluctuations associated with seasonal patterns.

As you delve into the intricacies of market timing and seasonal trends in this chapter, you'll not only gain insights into the cyclical nature of markets but also acquire the skills to strategically position your investments based on these patterns. This chapter becomes your roadmap to recognizing favorable times, adapting to market cycles, and leveraging seasonal trends to enhance your investment outcomes. Get ready to navigate the dynamic landscape of the market with precision and timing expertise.

CHAPTER 15

Real Estate Investments for Diversification

In Chapter 15, we embark on a journey into the world of real estate investments—a dynamic avenue that goes beyond traditional asset classes. This chapter serves as your guide to exploring real estate as a strategic component of your investment portfolio, offering insights on the benefits of diversification and how to balance your overall investment strategy with property investments.

Exploring Real Estate as an Investment Avenue

Understanding the Appeal of Real Estate:

Real estate is more than just bricks and mortar; it's a tangible asset class with unique characteristics. In this section, explore the fundamental reasons why investors are drawn to real estate. From potential for capital appreciation to income generation through rental yields, understand the diverse ways in which real estate can contribute to your investment portfolio.

Types of Real Estate Investments:

Real estate offers a spectrum of investment opportunities beyond traditional residential properties. Delve into various types of real estate investments, including commercial real estate, retail properties, industrial spaces, and real estate investment trusts (REITs). Understand the distinct advantages and considerations associated with each type, allowing you to tailor your real estate strategy to your investment goals.

Factors Influencing Real Estate Market Dynamics:

The real estate market is influenced by a myriad of factors, from economic indicators to local demographics. Gain insights into the dynamics that shape the real estate market, including interest rates, population trends, and economic cycles. Understanding these factors equips you with the knowledge to make informed decisions within the real estate investment landscape.

Balancing Your Portfolio with Property Investments

A. Diversification Benefits of Real Estate:

Diversification is a cornerstone of sound investment strategy, and real estate plays a unique role in this context. Explore the diversification benefits of incorporating real estate into your portfolio. Understand how real estate's low correlation with traditional asset classes can enhance the overall risk-return profile of your investment portfolio.

B. Risk Management in Real Estate Investing:

While real estate offers diversification benefits, it also comes with its own set of risks. Learn how to effectively manage and mitigate risks associated with real estate investments. From market risk to property-specific considerations, this section provides strategies for conducting thorough due diligence and safeguarding your real estate portfolio.

C. Practical Considerations for Real Estate Investing:

Real estate investing requires a strategic approach. Dive into practical considerations, including financing options, property management, and market timing. Whether you're considering direct property ownership or exploring REITs, this section equips you with the tools to navigate the intricacies of real estate investing.

As you navigate the realm of real estate investments in this chapter, you'll not only gain a comprehensive understanding of the unique characteristics of this asset class but also discover how to strategically integrate real estate into your investment portfolio. This chapter becomes your roadmap to exploring the opportunities, managing the risks, and leveraging the diversification benefits that real estate offers to enhance your overall investment strategy. Get ready to diversify your portfolio and unlock the potential of real estate as a dynamic component of your wealth-building journey.

CHAPTER 16

Retirement Planning for Young Professionals

In Chapter 16, we embark on a crucial exploration tailored for young professionals—a roadmap for early retirement and strategies for building wealth that lasts a lifetime. This chapter serves as your comprehensive guide to navigating the complexities of retirement planning, ensuring that your financial journey is not just secure but strategically positioned for early and lasting retirement.

Creating a Roadmap for Early Retirement

i.   Setting Early Retirement Goals:

For young professionals, the dream of early retirement is both ambitious and attainable. In this section, learn how to set clear and achievable early retirement goals. Understand the importance of defining your retirement lifestyle, estimating future expenses, and aligning your financial plan with the timeline for early retirement.

ii. Power of Compound Growth:

Time is your greatest asset in early retirement planning. Explore the power of compound growth and how starting early allows your investments to accumulate exponentially over time. Understand how strategic investment decisions, such as asset allocation and consistent contributions, can maximize the compounding effect on your retirement savings.

iii. Smart Savings and Investment Strategies:

Efficient savings and investment strategies are pivotal for early retirement success. Dive into techniques such as automatic savings, employer-sponsored retirement plans, and tax-advantaged accounts. Explore investment vehicles that offer a balance between risk and return, aligning with your risk tolerance and early retirement goals.

Strategies for Building Wealth that Lasts a Lifetime

- *Creating a Diversified Retirement Portfolio:*

A well-diversified retirement portfolio is essential for longevity. Explore the principles of diversification across asset classes, including equities, bonds, and alternative investments. Understand how a diversified portfolio can help manage risk and optimize returns, providing a solid foundation for a lasting retirement.

- *Incorporating Real Estate and Alternative Investments:*

Beyond traditional investment vehicles, consider the inclusion of real estate and alternative investments in your retirement strategy. Delve into the unique benefits and considerations associated with real estate, private equity, and other alternative assets. Learn how these investments can enhance diversification and contribute to long-term wealth building.

- *Tax-Efficient Retirement Withdrawal Strategies:*

Strategic withdrawal planning is crucial for sustaining wealth throughout retirement. Explore tax-efficient withdrawal strategies, including Roth conversions, systematic withdrawal plans, and optimizing your distributions from different types of retirement accounts. Understand how to minimize tax implications and make the most of your retirement income.

As you navigate through the intricacies of retirement planning for young professionals in this chapter, you'll not only gain the knowledge to create a roadmap for early retirement but also acquire the strategies to build wealth that lasts a lifetime. This chapter becomes your ally in forging a path towards financial independence, guiding you to make informed decisions that align with your aspirations for an early and secure retirement. Get ready to embark on a journey where your financial future is not just a destination but a lifelong pursuit of prosperity and fulfillment.

CHAPTER 17

Advanced Trading Strategies

Welcome to Chapter 17, a deep dive into the realm of advanced trading strategies. This chapter is designed to equip you with the knowledge and skills needed to navigate sophisticated investment approaches such as options trading and day trading. Learn how to harness these strategies effectively while mitigating risks and optimizing your investment outcomes.

Options Trading: Unlocking Strategic Possibilities

Understanding Options Basics:

Options trading is a dynamic strategy that opens new dimensions for investors. In this section, delve into the fundamentals of options trading, understanding concepts such as calls, puts, strike prices, and expiration dates. Gain insights into how options can be utilized for speculation, income generation, and risk management.

Advanced Options Strategies:

Explore advanced options trading strategies that go beyond simple calls and puts. From straddles and strangles to iron condors and butterflies, understand how these strategies allow you to capitalize on market volatility, hedge your positions, and potentially generate income in various market conditions.

Risks and Rewards of Options Trading:

While options trading offers strategic possibilities, it also involves inherent risks. Delve into the risks and rewards of options trading, understanding how leverage amplifies both potential gains and losses. Learn risk management techniques to safeguard your portfolio while exploring the advanced opportunities presented by options.

Day Trading Fundamentals:

Day trading involves making intraday trades to capitalize on short-term market movements. In this section, explore the fundamentals of day trading, including technical analysis, chart patterns, and intraday indicators. Gain insights into the unique challenges and opportunities presented by the fast-paced nature of day trading.

Advanced Day Trading Strategies:

Dive into advanced day trading strategies that go beyond basic intraday techniques. From momentum trading to reversal patterns, understand how to identify high-probability setups and execute well-timed trades. Explore the use of algorithmic trading and automated strategies to enhance your efficiency as a day trader.

Risk Mitigation in Day Trading:

Day trading comes with inherent risks, and effective risk mitigation is paramount. Learn how to manage risk in day trading through techniques such as setting stop-loss orders, position sizing, and avoiding emotional decision-making.

Understand the importance of maintaining discipline and adhering to a well-defined trading plan.

As you delve into the advanced trading strategies presented in this chapter, you'll not only expand your toolkit as an investor but also gain the skills to navigate the complexities of options trading and day trading with confidence. This chapter serves as your guide to unlocking strategic possibilities while maintaining a disciplined and risk-aware approach. Get ready to elevate your trading skills and explore the advanced tactics that can potentially enhance your investment journey.

CHAPTER 18

Mastering Cryptocurrency Investments

In Chapter 18, we embark on an exploration of the dynamic and ever-evolving world of cryptocurrency investments. This chapter serves as your comprehensive guide to navigating the intricacies of digital assets, providing insights into the unique characteristics of cryptocurrencies and strategies for integrating them into your investment portfolio.

Navigating the World of Digital Assets

Understanding Cryptocurrencies:

Cryptocurrencies represent a paradigm shift in the world of finance. In this section, delve into the foundational concepts of cryptocurrencies, including blockchain technology, decentralized networks, and cryptographic principles. Gain insights into the origins of cryptocurrencies, with a focus on the groundbreaking emergence of Bitcoin and the subsequent evolution of the crypto landscape.

Types of Cryptocurrencies:

The cryptocurrency ecosystem is diverse, comprising thousands of digital assets beyond Bitcoin. Explore different types of cryptocurrencies, including altcoins, tokens, and stablecoins. Understand the unique features and use cases of prominent cryptocurrencies such as Ethereum, Ripple, Litecoin, and others that have garnered attention in the digital asset space.

Market Dynamics and Volatility:

Cryptocurrency markets are known for their volatility and 24/7 trading. Delve into the market dynamics of cryptocurrencies, exploring factors that influence price movements, liquidity, and market sentiment. Understand the role of external factors, including regulatory developments, technological advancements, and macroeconomic trends in shaping the cryptocurrency landscape.

Integrating Cryptocurrencies into Your Investment Portfolio

- *Benefits and Risks of Cryptocurrency Investments:*

Cryptocurrencies offer unique benefits, including potential high returns and portfolio diversification. However, they also come with inherent risks, including market volatility and regulatory uncertainties. Explore the benefits and risks of cryptocurrency investments, allowing you to make informed decisions about their role in your portfolio.

- *Strategies for Investing in Cryptocurrencies:*

Developing a strategic approach is crucial when venturing into cryptocurrency investments. Explore different investment strategies, from long-term "HODLing" to active trading and tactical allocation. Understand the importance of conducting thorough research, managing risk, and staying informed about market trends to optimize your cryptocurrency investment strategy.

- *Security and Storage of Digital Assets:*

Security is paramount in the world of cryptocurrencies. Learn about best practices for securing your digital assets, including the use of hardware wallets, secure exchanges, and private key management. Understand the importance of staying vigilant against potential cyber threats and scams prevalent in the digital asset space.

As you navigate through the intricacies of mastering cryptocurrency investments in this chapter, you'll not only gain a deep understanding of the digital asset landscape but also acquire the knowledge and skills needed to integrate cryptocurrencies into your broader investment portfolio. This chapter becomes your roadmap to exploring the opportunities, managing the risks, and leveraging the unique characteristics of cryptocurrencies in your pursuit of financial growth and innovation. Get ready to master the art of cryptocurrency investments and unlock the potential of this transformative asset class.

CHAPTER 19

Financial Wellness and Lifestyle Design

In Chapter 19, we embark on a transformative journey that transcends traditional financial planning. This chapter is dedicated to the synergy between financial wellness and lifestyle design—a holistic approach that goes beyond monetary considerations to align your financial goals with your deepest personal aspirations. Explore how intentional choices in your financial life can lead to a purposeful and fulfilling lifestyle.

Aligning Financial Goals with Personal Aspirations

Defining Your Life Vision:

Financial wellness begins with a clear understanding of your life vision. In this section, embark on a reflective journey to define your personal aspirations, values, and long-term vision. Understand how your financial goals can be woven into this broader tapestry, creating a roadmap for a life that aligns with your deepest desires.

Creating S.M.A.R.T Financial Goals:

Transform your aspirations into actionable and achievable financial goals by applying the S.M.A.R.T framework—Specific, Measurable, Achievable, Relevant, and Time-bound. Learn how to break down overarching objectives into tangible milestones, allowing you to track progress and celebrate achievements on your journey towards financial wellness.

The Interplay Between Money and Happiness:

Delve into the intricate relationship between money and happiness. Explore the concept of "enough" and how defining your sufficiency threshold can contribute to a sense of financial well-being. Understand the principles of mindful spending, intentional saving, and how aligning your financial decisions with your values can enhance your overall life satisfaction.

Designing a Lifestyle that Reflects Your Financial Success

Intentional Spending and Conscious Consumption:

Designing a lifestyle aligned with your financial success involves intentional spending and conscious consumption. Explore strategies for mindful budgeting, prioritizing spending based on values, and cultivating a sense of gratitude for the resources you have. Learn how to make intentional choices that resonate with your desired lifestyle.

Balancing Instant Gratification and Delayed Rewards:

Financial wellness often requires a delicate balance between instant gratification and delayed rewards. Understand the psychology of instant gratification and explore techniques for cultivating patience and discipline in your financial decisions. Learn how delayed rewards can contribute to long-term financial success and a more fulfilling lifestyle.

Adapting Your Lifestyle to Financial Milestones:

As you progress on your financial journey, milestones and life events will shape your path. Explore strategies for adapting your lifestyle to financial milestones, whether it's buying a home, starting a family, or transitioning into retirement. Understand how flexibility and adaptability play key roles in designing a lifestyle that evolves with your changing circumstances.

This chapter serves as your guide to the intersection of financial wellness and lifestyle design, providing practical insights and strategies to align your financial goals with your personal aspirations. It's not just about the numbers; it's about crafting a life that reflects your values, passions, and sense of purpose. Get ready to embark on a transformative journey where financial success becomes a means to design a lifestyle that brings joy, fulfillment, and a true sense of well-being.

CHAPTER 20

The Future of Investing – Emerging Trends

In Chapter 20, we embark on a forward-looking exploration of the financial landscape—an insightful journey into the future of investing. This chapter is dedicated to unraveling emerging trends, exploring futuristic investment opportunities, and anticipating the forces that will shape the financial markets in the years to come.

Exploring Futuristic Investment Opportunities

The Rise of Artificial Intelligence in Investing:

As technology continues to advance, artificial intelligence (AI) is reshaping the investment landscape. Delve into the role of AI in investing, from algorithmic trading and robo-advisors to machine learning-driven investment strategies. Understand how AI can enhance decision-making, analyze vast datasets, and adapt to evolving market conditions, opening new avenues for investors.

Blockchain and Decentralized Finance (DeFi):

Blockchain technology, beyond its association with cryptocurrencies, is ushering in a new era of decentralized finance (DeFi). Explore how blockchain enables trustless financial transactions, smart contracts, and the creation of decentralized applications. Understand the potential impact of DeFi on traditional banking and explore investment opportunities within this rapidly evolving ecosystem.

Sustainable and Impact Investing Evolution:

The movement towards sustainable and impact investing is not just a trend; it's a transformative force shaping the future of investments. Explore how environmental, social, and governance (ESG) considerations are becoming integral to investment decisions. Understand the evolution of sustainable investing, from screening practices to active engagement and how it aligns with the broader shift towards conscious capitalism.

Anticipating Trends that Will Shape the Future of the Financial Markets

Cryptocurrencies Beyond Speculation:

While cryptocurrencies started as speculative assets, their role is evolving beyond mere investments. Explore how cryptocurrencies are becoming means of exchange, stores of value, and even integral components of financial infrastructure. Anticipate trends in central bank digital currencies (CBDCs) and the potential integration of cryptocurrencies into mainstream financial systems.

Climate Change and Investment Strategies:

Climate change is not just an environmental concern; it's a significant factor shaping investment strategies. Delve into how the financial industry is adapting to climate-related risks and opportunities. Explore the rise of green finance, sustainable bonds, and how investors are integrating climate considerations into portfolio management.

The Role of Big Data and Predictive Analytics:

Big data and predictive analytics are becoming indispensable tools for investors. Explore how the analysis of vast datasets, coupled with machine learning algorithms, is revolutionizing investment decision-making. Understand how predictive analytics can provide insights into market trends, consumer behavior, and economic indicators, empowering investors to make more informed and data-driven choices.

As you navigate through the future of investing in this chapter, you'll gain a strategic foresight into the trends and opportunities that will define the financial landscape. This chapter becomes your lens into the dynamic forces shaping the future, providing you with the knowledge and insights to stay ahead in the ever-evolving world of investments. Get ready to embrace the future of investing, where innovation, sustainability, and technology converge to create new frontiers for financial growth and prosperity.

CONCLUSION

Your Ongoing Journey to Financial Mastery

Congratulations on reaching the conclusion of this comprehensive guide, "Mastering Investing for Starters: 2024 Insights." Your journey into the intricate world of investing has been a transformative exploration, equipping you with knowledge, strategies, and insights to navigate the complexities of the financial landscape.

As you stand at the intersection of the knowledge gained from these pages, remember that your journey to financial mastery is an ongoing and dynamic process. Here, in the conclusion, we reinforce key principles and provide guidance for the road ahead.

Reflect on Your Financial Goals:

Take a moment to reflect on the financial goals you've set throughout this guide. Whether it's early retirement, building a diversified portfolio, or embracing emerging trends, these goals are the compass that guides your financial journey. Regularly reassess and refine them as your life evolves.

Continuous Learning and Adaptation:

The financial landscape is ever-changing, influenced by economic shifts, technological advancements, and global events. Embrace a mindset of continuous learning. Stay informed about emerging trends, technological innovations, and global economic developments. A commitment to staying informed positions you to adapt and thrive in any financial environment.

Diversify Strategically:

Diversification remains a cornerstone of successful investing. As you navigate the markets, consider the lessons learned about asset allocation, risk management, and the benefits of a well-diversified portfolio. Continually reassess your portfolio to ensure it aligns with your risk tolerance, financial goals, and the evolving market landscape.

Embrace Technological Advances:

Technology is a driving force in the financial world, from automated trading strategies to the rise of cryptocurrencies. Embrace technological advances and leverage them to your advantage. Explore opportunities presented by artificial intelligence, blockchain, and other innovations that can enhance your investment approach.

Stay Mindful of Your Values:

In the pursuit of financial success, it's crucial to remain mindful of your values. Whether it's sustainable and impact investing, conscious consumption, or aligning your lifestyle with your financial well-being, your values shape the decisions you make. Let them be the guiding principles that bring purpose to your financial journey.

Seek Professional Advice:

Consider seeking the guidance of financial professionals as you progress on your journey. Financial advisors, tax experts, and legal professionals can provide valuable insights tailored to your unique circumstances. Their expertise can be instrumental in making informed decisions and optimizing your financial strategy.

Community and Support:

Engage with a community of like-minded individuals who share your financial aspirations. Interactive forums, local meet-ups, and online communities can offer support, insights, and networking opportunities. Collaborating with others on similar journeys enhances your learning experience and provides a valuable support system.

In closing, your ongoing journey to financial mastery is not just about accumulating wealth—it's about creating a life of purpose, fulfillment, and resilience. As you apply the principles and strategies outlined in this guide, remember that financial mastery is a holistic pursuit that integrates knowledge, values, and adaptability.

May your financial journey be marked by success, wisdom, and the fulfillment of your deepest aspirations. This conclusion marks not an end but a continuation—an invitation to embrace the ongoing adventure that is your journey to financial mastery. Safe travels and best wishes on the road ahead!

APPENDIX

Resources for Continuous Learning

Congratulations on completing "Mastering Investing for Starters: 2024 Insights." As you embark on your ongoing journey to financial mastery, this appendix provides a curated list of resources to support your continuous learning. Whether you're looking for in-depth books, reliable websites, or cutting-edge tools, these resources will serve as valuable companions on your path to staying informed and empowered in the ever-evolving world of finance.

Recommended Books:

1. "The Intelligent Investor" by Benjamin Graham: A timeless classic that explores the principles of value investing, providing insights into the mindset of a successful investor.

2. "A Random Walk Down Wall Street" by Burton Malkiel: A comprehensive guide to understanding different investment strategies, from passive investing to behavioral finance.

3. "Common Stocks and Uncommon Profits" by Philip Fisher: An insightful exploration of qualitative analysis and a deep dive into understanding businesses for long-term investment.

4. "Thinking, Fast and Slow" by Daniel Kahneman: A Nobel laureate's exploration of the psychological factors influencing decision-making and their impact on investment choices.

5. "The Little Book That Still Beats the Market" by Joel Greenblatt: An accessible guide to value investing principles, offering a systematic approach to stock selection.

Websites for Ongoing Education:

1. Investopedia (www.investopedia.com): A comprehensive online resource covering a wide range of financial topics, from investing basics to advanced strategies.

2. Morningstar (www.morningstar.com): A platform offering in-depth analysis on stocks, mutual funds, and ETFs, along with valuable tools for portfolio management.

3. Seeking Alpha (www.seekingalpha.com): A community-driven platform where investors share insights, analysis, and commentary on stocks and investment trends.

4. Khan Academy (www.khanacademy.org): A free educational platform offering courses on finance, economics, and investment principles.

5. The Motley Fool (www.fool.com): A multimedia financial services company providing investment insights, stock recommendations, and educational content.

Tools for Investment Analysis:

Yahoo Finance (finance.yahoo.com): A comprehensive financial platform offering real-time stock quotes, news, and a range of analytical tools.

1. StockCharts (www.stockcharts.com): A resource for technical analysis, providing advanced charting tools and insights into market trends.

2. QuantConnect (www.quantconnect.com): A platform for algorithmic trading, allowing users to develop, test, and deploy trading strategies using historical data.

3. Bloomberg Terminal (www.bloomberg.com): A professional-grade platform providing real-time financial data, news, and analytics widely used by financial professionals.

4. Personal Capital (www.personalcapital.com): A financial planning tool that aggregates all your financial accounts, providing a holistic view of your financial situation.

Exclusive Online Resources for Continuous Updates:

1. CFA Institute (www.cfainstitute.org): Access resources, research publications, and webinars from the Chartered Financial Analyst (CFA) Institute.

2. MIT OpenCourseWare (ocw.mit.edu): Explore finance courses from the Massachusetts Institute of

Technology for in-depth learning on various financial topics.

3. Financial Times (www.ft.com): Stay updated with global financial news, analysis, and insights from one of the leading financial publications.

4. Barron's (www.barrons.com): A premier source for market insights, investment recommendations, and analysis of economic trends.

5. TED Talks - Finance Playlist (www.ted.com): Explore TED Talks on finance, economics, and investment, featuring thought-provoking discussions by industry experts.

As you utilize these resources, remember that continuous learning is a cornerstone of financial mastery. Stay curious, explore new ideas, and adapt your knowledge to the evolving financial landscape. The journey to financial wisdom is ongoing, and these resources are here to support your growth and success. Happy learning!

EPILOGUE

A Letter to Future Investors

Dear Future Investor,

As you hold these words in your hands, you are standing at the threshold of a profound journey—one that transcends the pages of this guide and ventures into the dynamic world of finance. The insights, strategies, and knowledge within these chapters serve as both a compass and a launching pad for your endeavors.

In embarking on your investment journey, envision it not as a mere pursuit of wealth but as a strategic voyage toward financial empowerment, wisdom, and ultimately, a life of purpose. The path ahead is filled with opportunities, challenges, and moments of profound growth.

Embrace the Learning Curve:

The world of investing is expansive, dynamic, and ever-evolving. As you navigate its intricacies, embrace the learning curve. Every challenge you encounter is an opportunity to refine your skills, expand your understanding, and emerge as a more seasoned investor.

Cultivate a Mindset of Resilience:

Resilience is the currency of successful investors. Markets will fluctuate, unforeseen events will arise, and decisions may not always yield the expected outcomes. In these moments, let resilience be your anchor. Learn from setbacks, adapt to change, and press forward with a steadfast commitment to your financial goals.

Balance Aspiration with Prudence:

Your aspirations are the driving force behind your journey, but balance them with prudence. Distinguish between speculation and informed decision-making. Seek opportunities aligned with your risk tolerance and financial objectives. The art of investing lies in finding the equilibrium between ambition and prudent risk management.

Harness the Power of Diversification:

Diversification is your ally in building a robust and resilient portfolio. Spread your investments across different asset classes, industries, and geographic regions. This strategy not only mitigates risk but also positions you to capitalize on a spectrum of opportunities, ensuring your financial journey is well-rounded and adaptive.

Stay Adaptable to Change:

The financial landscape is dynamic, shaped by technological advancements, global events, and economic shifts. Stay adaptable to change. Embrace emerging trends, leverage technological tools, and remain vigilant to the evolving opportunities that will define the future of investing.

Connect with a Community of Learners:

You are not alone on this journey. Connect with a community of like-minded individuals who share your enthusiasm for financial growth. Engage in discussions, seek mentorship, and contribute to the collective wisdom of a thriving community. The exchange of ideas and experiences will enrich your learning and propel you forward.

Invest with Purpose:

Beyond the pursuit of financial gains, invest with purpose. Consider the impact of your decisions on your life, the lives of others, and the broader world. Align your investments with your values, and let your financial journey reflect not just wealth accumulation but a meaningful and purpose-driven pursuit.

Dear Future Investor, the path you tread is one of continuous growth, adaptation, and discovery. As you navigate the ever-changing currents of the financial world, may you find not only financial success but a profound sense of fulfillment, wisdom, and purpose.

Your journey is not marked by a destination but by the ongoing evolution of your financial mastery. As you step into the future, may your endeavors be guided by prudence, resilience, and the unwavering belief that your journey is a testament to the infinite possibilities that lie ahead.

Wishing you a future filled with financial prosperity, fulfillment, and the realization of your most ambitious dreams.

With best wishes,

An Advocate of Your Financial Success